BULLET JOURNAL

170 DOT-GRID PAGES

North Mountain®

ISBN-13: 978-1986690676
ISBN-10: 1986690679

THIS BELONGS TO:

Made in United States
Orlando, FL
14 August 2023

36067009R00096